Angels, Saints, and Spirits

THROUGH HER OWN EXPERIENCE

KAREN KAZIMER SHOCKLEY

ISBN 979-8-88751-675-2 (paperback)
ISBN 979-8-88751-676-9 (digital)

Christian Faith Publishing
832 Park Avenue
Meadville, PA 16335
www.christianfaithpublishing.com

Printed in the United States of America

Introduction

We have all heard of angels that save you, saints that you can pray to, and spirits that come and visit. Angels are the ones that get their wings when a bell rings. Saints are people the Catholic church has deemed "super holy with a direct line to God." Spirits pretty much cover any other physical phenomena that cannot be explained. All of these beings seem far away from daily life. But to me, they *are* my daily life. Countless times, the unexplained has occurred, unless one wants to accept the existence of these individuals. This book presents my own experiences where I prefer to believe in fairies or any other being that I can't always see clearly but know is there.

As you read this book, please take the opportunity to reflect on events in your lives that seemed to have no explanation. You may want to jot these times down on the pages at the end of this book. This journey belongs to all of us.

To Believe or Not to Believe

My first story concerns Saint Anthony. Now, as many of you may know, saints have special duties. St. Christopher kept Jesus safe, and many people carried his medal in their cars so that they, too, could share in this protection. And of course, there is St. Jude, the Saint of the Impossible, whose hospital for critically ill children is aptly named; his job is to watch over the patients. And there is St. Anthony, the patron saint of lost things.

It is St. Anthony who plays a large part of this story. More than once, someone in our family has asked St. Anthony to aid them in locating a lost item, but my most vivid recollection is of a summer day at the beach. For those of you who have been to the Outer Banks of North Carolina, you know that beaches can be crowded, almost blanket to blanket with sunbathers getting their rays.

Now, my older daughter, Beth, around ten at the time, had prudently taken off her rings and necklaces prior to going into the water. Lots of things can get loose and fall off in the midst of all those waves! And to make extra sure her valuables were safe, she buried them in the sand just under a corner of our blanket. After a wonderful, fun-filled day, we all left for dinner.

After dinner, I heard the "uh-oh" from Beth, which *never* means good news. She had just remembered her jewelry. When she said, "Mom, what should I do?" I replied that we should say a short prayer to St. Anthony and go back to the beach. Now I have no actual proof that there is even a St. Anthony, or that he was listening, or, even if he was, if he designed to help. My little girl, though, went to those acres and acres of sandy beach where every patch of sand looks like every other patch. She went right to the place where her jewelry was buried and dug it up. Now, she may have subconsciously recognized geographic signs such as the way the dune plants grew, or the buoys were bouncing, but for me, this was nothing short of a miracle. I asked her how she knew where her jewelry was, and "she just knew." Thank you, St. Anthony.

I Do Believe

The beach, in fact, is a very good place to have your guardian angel with you. For those of you who aren't familiar with guardian angels, these are beings whose job it is to take especially good care of their assigned person. Your guardian angel is the one who guides your car a little to the right so that the car on your left misses you by inches when it passes you at 40 mph over the speed limit and wanders into your lane. Your guardian angel is also the one who urges you to buckle your seat belt (even if you normally do not) just before the car in front of you stops suddenly, making your seat belt the only reason you don't go flying through the windshield as you slam on the brakes.

Anyway, as I was saying, the beach can be a very dangerous place. There are jellyfish to sting you, waves to knock you down, and riptides to pull you under, just to name a few such hazards. It was at just such a beach at about six in the evening that my brother was watching his ten-year-old son, John, dig a large hole in the sand. This seemed on the surface to be a reasonably safe activity. The hole was nowhere near the water. Instead, it was positioned at the bottom of the dunes that divide the beach from the houses that fronted it. And to make extra sure this was a safe activity, my brother sat no more than two feet away, enjoying the sand and the sun and watching the waves come in.

This was a very peaceful scene, at about six in the evening, well after almost all the sun worshippers had called it a day. So there my brother sat with his young son digging and digging and digging. As he dug further, he climbed into the hole to be able to *really* make it deep. Still, everything seemed safe and sane.

And then…there was just one shovel full of sand too much on the sand around the hole. Before anyone knew what was happening, the water rushed in from the bottom of the dugout. What had two seconds before been a nice, tranquil scene turned into a battle of life and death. The water had gotten hold of John and was tossing and turning him in the water, back and forth and up and down and every which way you can imagine. My brother frantically grabbed for him but could not even begin to reach him. One of the remaining bathers called 911, but even as they could hear the sirens coming toward them, no one was sure that my nephew would be rescued in time.

Then (just like in the movies) a white-haired man approached from down the beach. He appeared to just have been walking along. He sized up the situation, strode over to the hole, and with one quick motion, pulled my nephew to safety. And just like that, it was over. It turns out this man had been guarding and managing beach safety for quite a number of years. He remarked that many people were unaware of the danger of drowning in just such holes.

The paramedics then duly checked out John, pronounced him fine (except for perhaps a newly developed fear of water holes), and left. My brother then turned back to where the rescuer had been standing—but he was gone. Just like that. No man walking down the beach anywhere, and no one heading up the dunes. It was just like he knew to be in the right place at the right time to perform his job and then disappear, most likely to another quick save. Now everyone might not call this miraculous, but you can be quite sure my brother and I do! And just to be on the safe side, there is no more hole digging while standing in a hole anywhere—beach or not.

The Just-in-Time Beach Angel

And I have yet another opportunity to thank a guardian angel. This time, again at the beach, my twenty-year-old daughter developed a skin rash. At first, this seemed like a normal allergic reaction to something akin to poison ivy. Something that could be easily remedied by calamine lotion and time and lots of water. Whenever anyone around me is ill, I feel obligated to counsel them to take a bath and drink lots of water. I mean, you want to make sure you're clean just in case you *do* have to go to the doctor's office, and a little water never hurt anyone, right?

Anyway, the next morning my daughter woke me up. Not only is the rash worse, but she felt like something was really wrong. We rushed to the Outer Banks medical clinic and, being a Monday, of course it was packed. We signed in, and as we were sitting there we could literally watch Julia's skin break out in more and more and more hives. Not being medically astute as to the dangers of a quickly spreading rash, we were actually taking wagers on what part of her body would be covered first.

After an hour of this phenomenon and when my daughter was almost completely covered in spots, she went to the desk to say that perhaps she needed immediate care. It happened to be at a time when lots of people were making the same query at the desk, so she was given the standard "we are helping everyone as soon as we can, please take your seat."

She did, and half an hour later, she was finally called in to the examining room. I knew that when the nurse came back out to the waiting room to tell me I might want to join my daughter that the news was not good. Later on, I viewed this request as extraordinarily good as well as timely.

At about the exact time my daughter was asked by the doctor to open her mouth, her throat began to swell. Immediate action was taken, and although we had a tense minute or two when my daughter still felt her throat closing, we survived just fine. I still have an alternate picture in the back of my mind. This is one of what could have happened. Only five minutes more of waiting in the lobby could have found Julia collapsing on the waiting room floor, unable to breathe with people trying to revive her but hampered by not knowing of the rapidly blocking airway. I call this "just in time" angel action.

Note: Julia had one more allergic attack when we were at home and on familiar territory. She did have to be rushed to the hospital in an ambulance. We never did find the cause of the allergy, but she carries her EpiPen and trusts that someone is watching over her every day.

Guardian Angels—
Everyone Has One

Even golden agers have guardian angels. My parents, in their sixties at the time of this story, were performing their annual journey from their home in Cleveland, Ohio, to mine in the northern part of Virginia.

My father, for some unknown reason still, did not stop at the normal watering hole to fill up the gas tank and purchase any needed supplies (read snacks). My mom was somewhat concerned, but each time she brought up the state of their gas supply, my dad would simply say, "It's okay." Things went on this way for mile after mile until my father could no longer ignore the telltale blinking light that reads "low gas." Finally deciding to turn off the highway, he was lucky enough to be able to coast down the off-ramp as the last of the gas disappeared. Meanwhile, my mom began saying her favorite prayer, the "Hail Mary," hoping against hope that they would arrive *somewhere* safely.

Once again, an angel must have been listening because the vehicle *directly* behind them pulled over, stopped, and asked if they needed gas. It seems the driver always kept a spare container of gas in his pickup truck. He poured his gas into my parents' tank and then followed them to a gas station where they filled up his container as well as their car. My mom concluded the event by saying one more "thank you, Hail Mary," and they were safely on their way, just as if the whole scenario had been planned.

Note: Do *not* try this at home.

Some People Learn
the Hard Way

When I say, "don't try this at home," I really mean it because of course, I did try it. This time it was just myself and my son, who was eight at the time. We were making the same trip from Ohio to Virginia. It was somewhat later in the day, however, bordering on night. And to avoid an hour-long backup on the turnpike, I decided to take a new way, which had me on a relatively new highway about eleven thirty at night.

Here I am, a theoretically responsible parent, driving down an unfamiliar road, late in the evening with my young son. I did happen to notice that the gas tank seemed to be rapidly emptying (I think it goes from a quarter tank to zero much more quickly than it takes to traverse any of the other quarters on the dial). So I was faced with the same dilemma most parents face every day. Do I stop the car *now* and wake my child up—which could prompt anything from just drowsiness to pleas for candy, ice cream, a drink, and the bathroom. You can see that in this instance waking the child is not a preferred option.

I made the only sensible choice and that was to drive a little longer. And a little longer and yet more. It is now midnight, and I am on a "new to me" highway where it is very, very dark. And as I tried to find a gas station, I realized that this highway is not the turnpike where there are rest stops and gas stations open all night long. This is just a road. And I am going down this road after midnight on a Sunday. I started to take exits where it says "gas" and learned that there are not many gas stations open in the middle of the Midwest after midnight on a Sunday. And no, you can't just put in your credit card and buy gas by yourself as you can during the day; I tried. So each time I would get back on the highway, I'd go to the next exit and then try to determine if I should take the risk to look for gas. If I did find an open gas station, my troubles would be over, and I would move back over the good parent side again. However, if the gas station was closed, I would have used up more of the precious fuel.

Now for some reason, while all this was going through my head, I wasn't panicking. Really and truly, I thought everything would be okay. And then, there it was—five miles across the state line—in big neon letters, "Truck Stop." I took the exit, and just like my father, I cruised down the off-ramp until I was about fifty yards from my goal before coming to a complete stop. My son was up by this time, asking why the car was stopped in the middle of the road. I told him it was just resting and turned the key. Sure enough, the car apparently had been sitting just right so more gas went to the part of the tank that fed the engine, and we were going forward. We got to the gas station and thankfully filled up. I didn't even mind that all the pumps except high test were locked up. True to form, we then got our water, a restroom break, and ice cream. And all this seemed like a dream. But it really happened to me. And I sincerely thank whoever was watching over me and my child that night.

A Grandmother's Prayer Is Answered, and a Child Is Born

The time was 1982, and my husband was in the air force on duty in Korea. He left his pregnant wife, me, and our fourteen-month-old baby behind. I was living at the time in Virginia where my only close relative was my husband's brother and sister-in-law.

As the time of the forecasted due date drew near, my mother joined me to help with logistics. This was the plan:

- I would go into labor.
- When the pains got to be close together—say seven minutes apart—I would call my sister-in-law, a neonatal nurse.
- My sister-in-law would drive to my house in her car and then take me to the hospital in my newer car.
- My mom would watch my toddler.

Seemed like a good plan, assuming I followed the normal labor path, my sister-in-law was reachable and that her very old car was working.

Oh, one other thing. My car was a manual shift, and, in the event my mother had to drive me to the hospital, that is the car she would be using.

My mother is sometimes a worrier and was afraid that if things did not go according to plan, *she* would have to drive me to the hospital. Now driving a pregnant woman to the hospital is not anyone's vision of a good time, but to complicate things, my mother had not driven a car with manual transmission in over twenty years. And with my husband in the military, we had to go to the closest military hospital, which was approximately forty-five minutes away.

So my mother prayed and prayed and prayed that she would not have to drive a woman in labor and her granddaughter to a hospital forty-five minutes away on a major beltway (did I mention we lived in a suburb of Washington, DC) in a manual transmission car.

Well, Grandma got her wish. She did not have to experience that potentially perilous drive. Instead, my daughter began her journey into our world after two labor pains and the breaking of my water.

I went to the bathroom (it was a large one) since I figured that was the best thing to do. I also called to my mom that I didn't think I was going to make it to the hospital. Her very words were "Karen, what have you gotten me into this time?"

She called the hospital, and while she was on the line, my beautiful baby girl was born. My mom was kept busy between checking on me and talking to the nurse; since my daughter started crying we jointly determined things were all okay. My mom then called my sister-in-law and the ambulance.

The medical team arrived about one minute before my sister-in-law. When she got the news that the baby was coming, she jumped into her car and pushed the pedal to the metal. I think she made the twenty-minute drive in less than ten minutes. She pulled up outside of our home, and her car died. Forever. It gave its life so that I could have my wonderful sister-in-law by my side as I went to the hospital.

The time was about two in the morning, and my first daughter had by now woken up to see what the excitement was all about. My mom told her, "Mommy is very busy now. You just sit right here on the couch and be very quiet." I believe children have a second sense about these things, and that is exactly what she did.

The paramedics announced that I was fine and delivered me to a hospital three minutes away (emergencies trump military requirements). I couldn't have made that trip without my calm, caring sister-in-law accompanying me. She knew just what I was thinking by reading my expression and assured me that she watched my baby until the hospital personnel appropriately tagged her as mine. While that was not an experience I would do again, I was very grateful that the home birth turned out well.

I am truly grateful for the following:

- My sister-in-law's car had one last ride in it and used it to help me.
- My mother did not have to experience a harrowing ride.
- And my wonderful baby girl was perfect.

Note: The Red Cross informed my husband that he had a baby girl; his mom called him and relayed the circumstances and, being a man, he had to say, "That wouldn't have happened had I been there! I would have gotten my wife to the hospital!" Oh, well, we have to let the "stronger sex" keep their delusions.

The Call Heard Four Hundred Miles Away!

As I relayed in the first chapter, I'm not truly sure whether there are angels living among us, spirits assisting us, or God orchestrating events. However, I have an unusual story concerning me and my dad. My dad and I have always been close. Although he was a man of few words, he always let his love be known by affectionate hugs and smiles. Whenever anyone gave him a present, he accepted it with wonder that someone would take the time and effort to give him something. It never mattered if it was something he truly liked, or that the tie he received coincidentally matched six other ones in his closet.

As my dad grew older, he began having minor strokes. He was given medication for them and was able to work until retirement age. Sometime after that, however, I woke at five in the morning on a Saturday to hear my dad calling me. His voice sounded exactly like the one he used when he was calling me to come down from my bedroom on the second floor. I was still in Virginia; he was in Ohio. I woke my husband to tell him what I heard. We decided that it was too early to call my parents just in case the voice I heard had truly been just a dream.

Well, being a Saturday, I soon became involved in the children's soccer practice, housekeeping, and other chores. I often thought about my dad but rationalized that if something had truly happened, I would have been called.

I was not called that day, but the next when I learned that at exactly five in the morning on Saturday, he had suffered a massive stroke. My mom and brother were "watching to see what happened," and when he had not moved in some time, they had taken him to the hospital. With everything going on, they were both busy until late in the evening and decided not to disturb me.

I truly wish that I would have called and comforted my dad (and suggested that he be taken to the hospital sooner). But at least I was notified right on time.

Note: My dad made a full recovery with the exception of a slight limp.

More Long-Distance Communication

My uncle had been dealing with cancer for several years, and the end was drawing near. He was in hospice with his wife by his side. As he knew the end was near, he kept reassuring my aunt that he would call her to let her know when he safely arrived at the end of his journey to the other side. She questioned him, "How can you possibly call me?" His response, "Don't worry, I know the number."

At the end of a long day sitting by her husband's side, my aunt went home to get some rest. As she lay there, and an hour or so later, she received a phone call. When she picked up the receiver, no one appeared to be there. We later learned from her daughter-in-law who was right by my uncle's side as he passed away that his death and the phone call coincided exactly in time.

The Bond Is Still Strong

As my father lay dying in his hospital bed, he was classified as a person in a nonresponsive state. The best I could figure out was that this wasn't exactly a coma but close to it. He didn't speak and only lay in bed with his eyes closed.

However, when I flew in from Virginia to see him, my mom spoke to my dad, "Honey, Karen's here. It's her birthday!"

My dad clearly responded with "Happy birthday to you, happy birthday to you, happy birthday to my 'Carin' for you' [his nickname for me—a play on the two phrases: 'Karen for you' and 'caring for you')." And then he went back to his nonresponsive state.

We also believed that God was calling him. He was having trouble breathing, and the medical staff tried to insert a breathing tube *five* times. He fought them off enough each time that they finally gave him. Three days later, my dad peacefully transitioned to his place in heaven.

Another Goodbye

I had a similar experience in my life with another person I truly loved. The time was approximately five months prior to our wedding. I spoke to my fiancée when he was at work on Tuesday, and he said that he was not feeling well, was going home early, and would not be at work the next day.

I refrained from calling him Tuesday and Wednesday, deciding I didn't want to take the chance of waking him.

On Thursday, though, I definitely decided something was wrong and tried to reach him, but it was with no results. As I was driving home with a colleague that afternoon, my cell phone rang with my fiancée's number showing. I didn't want to talk to him in the small confines of the car, so I decided to call him later.

And, anyway, just knowing he was well enough to call, put a warm, peaceful feeling in my heart. As things turned out, my love went home Tuesday night, got into bed, and passed away of a heart attack. No one investigated until Thursday afternoon when he didn't answer his phone and didn't come to work.

Once again, the mysterious had happened. They found Mike on Thursday, the afternoon I had received the call. I tried to check the exact time later, but both my brother and I checked my cell phone. I not only did not receive a call from Mike's phone that afternoon, I had not received a call from anyone. I still remember that incident warmly as my goodbye kiss.

And More Helpful Spirits

My son was in seventh grade at the impressionable age of thirteen. I may mention that adolescents are not known either for their common sense or the ability to foresee the possible consequences of their actions. However, not even I would have seen this story coming!

It was a bright, sunny afternoon in November. My son and his friends were in our neighborhood, retuning from the local 7-Eleven. They had purchased a box of candy called Jujubes—of a substance much like goomie worms. As cars went by, they determined (and remember my mention of no foresight) that it would be fun to throw Jujubes at passing cars.

Now Jujubes weigh less than an oz and may fill the space of a nickel if you flattened it out. These drivers were in no danger of swerving off the road, having their windshield cracked, or even having their car stained by the colored candy. With all this in mind, one driver who evidently didn't appreciate his car being pelted with candy of any kind just stopped his car. My son's friends who were either smarter or faster thinking started to run as fast as they could away from the stopped car.

My son, however, was evidently too stunned to move. I should mention that at this age, he was already six feet tall, so it is possible that he was mistaken for a much more mature person. The passenger, a large man draped in gold chains and covered in tattoos, proceeded to smack my son on the side of the head so hard that he collapsed. The car sped off, neighbors called the paramedics; he was checked out as "fine" and taken home.

My son suffered terrible headaches, though, and as these continued for over a week, we visited the doctor. The result of a scan showed that not only had my son been knocked unconscious, but that he had suffered a fractured skull as well as a subdural hematoma (bleeding inside the brain).

He was taken to Children's hospital; I was told he would most likely need brain surgery. Children's was a teaching hospital where he was a great example of someone who suffered a skull fracture with internal bleeding and lived without any intervention. The night after the accident, he could have very well left us. However, since he had survived the night, the blood was being absorbed into the brain tissue, and his skull was healing nicely, the decision was made to not take any action. Nature was doing just fine on its own.

I was so thankful that

- my son survived the first night;
- brain surgery was not required (okay, it was not required because we waited too long, but it still removed the chance of a lot of complications); and
- through the grace of God, my son fully recovered.

Note: My son progressed rapidly to full health, although he did get tired of performing tests for the doctors—can you touch your two fingers together, can you stand up and hold out your arms, etc. At one point, he informed me he knew all the tests by heart and if he could just stay and do them at home.

One More Happy Ending

One year later, on the same school holiday, my son had another brush with danger. This time it was all his own doing. Fancying himself a world-class skateboarder, he tried a quarter loop, left the board, and landed on his ankle.

We have yet another trip to the emergency room; it was determined that he had incurred a very bad sprain, and his ankle was wrapped appropriately. During the next two weeks, my son insisted repeatedly that his ankle had been broken. Despite our best efforts to convince him otherwise, he would not go to school and spend the next week keeping his ankle still and traveling up and down the hall between bedroom, bathroom, and kitchen by laying on his skateboard and pushing himself along.

It was then that I got a call from the doctor. It turns out there are something called "wet x-rays" that do not show things as clearly as what I would suppose are "dry x-rays." I was asked to bring my son in for a cast as he had a broken ankle.

The doctor showed me where the ankle had been broken clean through. Had the break been seen the day it happened, my son most likely would have screws holding his ankle together. Once again, fate (or whatever) smiled upon him. He had been keeping his ankle at the exactly correct position to heal. There was no need to rebreak the ankle and reposition it as normally would have been the case. My son received his walking cast, and a month or so later, it was good to go.

So thanks to the saint who watches over children or his guardian angel or the spirit that brings just plain good luck. As a mother, I will take all the help I can get.

Our Work on Earth Is Not Always Done

Not too long ago, a good friend of mine, Rick, contracted the dreaded COVID-19 disease. For weeks after his recovery, he had trouble breathing. We both brushed this off since problem breathing is known to be an unfortunate side effect of the disease. However, he kept getting worse and worse and worse.

One day I just happened to wake up early and went to see how Rick was doing. He asked me how he looked. I replied, "Like you are going to have a heart attack." (I had seen another friend of mine just before he had his heart attack.) Knowing in my heart that things were not good, I drove him to the emergency room. Until we got in the car, I had not realized how ill he was. He didn't want to drive!

We were very lucky. There was no one ahead of us at the ER. Of course, this might have been because it was six in the morning. He was taken immediately into the treatment room. Although the doctor had to run his many, many tests before he said anything, we finally learned that my friend had a pulmonary embolism. This is otherwise known as a blood clot in the lungs. Immediate action was taken; an ambulance arrived to take him to the best hospital in the area for this diagnosis. Before we left, the doctor told us that had we waited twenty-four hours to come in, my friend would indeed have died of a massive heart attack.

The hospital staff was very nice, but they decided to "wait and see" if the clot would dissolve on its own. It didn't, and the next day, the doctor performed surgery to remove the clot. Of course, a bad situation became worse when the first try at inserting the tube in the blood vessel didn't work. After much time and discomfort to the patient, the staff had to try a second area. The clot was successfully removed.

It was too early to start celebrating, however. We learned that the clot had damaged Rick's heart. First, the clot was sitting right on the heart. Second, apparently if one is not getting enough oxygen, the heart decides to pump harder to increase blood flow. If you have a blockage, the heart just wears itself out trying to self-help.

After the surgery, my friend still had extensive pain at the site of the first intubation. And the site kept getting more and more purple. The staff scheduled another scan, but, with one thing and another, determined that the hospital didn't have enough resources to perform the procedure that day. They waited until the next. And because this is the way things were going, it took two technicians and finally a doctor to perform the correct scan.

Rick went back to his room, still in pain. About forty-five minutes later, he is told he is going immediately into surgery. He didn't even change beds; they just wheeled him in his bed down to the operating room. There they repaired two places where the artery had been nicked as the tube was inserted. Everything was fine, once again, except for the attendant bruising. One of the doctors came for a visit when the patient was back in the hospital room. He remarked he "just had to see the patient that cheated death three times." It is going to take a year to fully recover, but he will, I'm sure. God still has work for Rick to do.

I'm thinking that, for sure, this must be true given the other close calls Rick has had during his lifetime. When he was a child, Rick slammed his arm through a glass door, cutting the artery and narrowly surviving the trip to the hospital. When Rick was a little older, he fell through the ice on a mostly frozen pond, walked home in quickly freezing clothes, but survived hypothermia. As an adult, he was thrown from the raft while white water rafting and became tangled in plants at the bottom. He was able to free himself and yes, had to recover from another bout of hypothermia. This same person lost control of his car at a track doing 120 mph and was stopped by the huge wall of tires placed there for just such an occasion. He walked away with a bruise on his arm from the air bag. I do feel a bit sorry for Rick's guardian angel. He has quite a job.

And Sometimes Our Work Is Finished Way Too Soon

My brother was taken from us at the age of sixty-three, quite premature to our way of thinking. He had had trouble breathing ever since contracting COVID, but this was attributed to just one of the side effects.

Eventually, several months later, he *really* couldn't breathe. He was admitted to the hospital; the doctors determined he had a tumor in his neck. He was discharged and scheduled for surgery in two weeks.

Four days later, Sam collapsed on the floor at home and once again is taken to the hospital. He is once again admitted; the results of a previous biopsy came in and he had not one, but three types of cancer in his throat area. I should probably also relate that my brother was a diabetic and occasionally suffered from a racing heart. Still, he was happy, and he felt good with the exception of the breathing problem.

A few days into the hospital stay, Sam suffered a massive heart attack and died. He was resuscitated after twenty minutes but never regained consciousness. A few days later, he passed away. I was able to be with him when he passed, and it was clear to me that his spirit had already left at the time of the heart attack. He was already in heaven, helping us along.

To a certain extent, the heart attack was a blessing. The cancerous tumors were fast growing, inoperable, and deadly. My brother would have died in less than two months, most likely with a lot of pain and suffering beforehand.

Sam was only sixty-three. But twenty-four months before he passed away, at age sixty-two, he retired. He just got a feeling that was the right thing to do. And so he spent the last part of his life doing things he loved, visiting friends, and helping people. I'm sure all of us would be grateful to "just have a feeling" listed to our heart.

As I look back on these stories and all the memories they invoke, I now believe more strongly than ever that there are forces in this world that influence our lives. By accepting their existence, we can embrace their actions and thank God for the gifts they are.

My Own Experiences

For those of you who read the Bible, it also contains references to angels and saints. Their job is clear—to help us succeed and protect us from evil. The following are taken from the King James Version of the Bible. You may want to refer to these passages as you contemplate your own experiences.

Bible verses about angels, saints, and spirits

> *To all that be in Rome, beloved of God, called to be saints: Grace to you and peace from God our Father, and the Lord Jesus Christ.*
> —Romans 1:7

> *Here is the patience of the saints: here are they that keep the commandments of God, and the faith of Jesus.*
> —Revelation 14:12

> *And another angel came and stood at the altar, having a golden censer; and there was given unto him much incense, that he should offer it with the prayers of all saints upon the golden altar which was before the throne.*
> —Revelation 8:3

> *The angel of the LORD encampeth round about them that fear him, and delivereth them.*
> —Psalm 34:7

> *For he shall give his angels charge over thee, to keep thee in all thy ways.*
> —Psalm 91:11

*And he shall send his angels with a great sound of a
trumpet, and they shall gather together his elect from the
four winds, from one end of heaven to the other.*
                                                    —Matthew 24:31

*Are they not all ministering spirits, sent forth to minister
for them who shall be heirs of salvation?*
                                                    —Hebrews 1:14

About the Author

As a Catholic, Karen Kazimer Shockley was raised with an almost overwhelming amount of religious input. Karen began a journey to use this information to bring religion to a place where it was real in her life. This process reached critical mass when she met a wonderful man who embodied the true Christian life, without structured religion. Through his influence, she began to recognize spiritual presences in her own life. Her goal is to share these experiences with others so that they, too, can achieve spiritual peace.

By day, Karen works in the computer field, performing tasks in almost every phase—including programming, training, and management. Karen has published several articles on the technical knowledge she gained. Karen would now like to share experiences from her heart.

Milton Keynes UK
Ingram Content Group UK Ltd.
UKHW012139131223
434291UK00001B/121

9 798887 516752